CONTENTS

Trinity Mirror Media

Compiled by Peter Grant
Sub-Editor: Vicky Andrews
Design: Zoe Bevan, Colin Harrison

Pictures courtesy of Liverpool Daily Post and Echo
Archive. With special thanks to Colin Hunt; the Kingham
family; and to Robin Bird for the use of the Bob Bird and
Keith Medley photographs.

Business Development Director: Mark Dickinson
Executive Editor: Ken Rogers
Senior Editor: Steve Hanrahan, Editor: Paul Dove
Senior Art Editor: Rick Cooke
Trinity Mirror Media Marketing Executive: Claire Brown
Sales and Marketing Manager: Elizabeth Morgan
Sales and Marketing Assistant: Karen Cadman

Printed by Pensord

ISBN 9 781906 802882

ALL ABOARD
Boarding the ferry to
New Brighton in 1960

A FERRY RIDE TO SEASIDE HEAVEN

NEW BRIGHTON, beloved of all our yesterdays, also has a promising tomorrow. By David Charters.

IT'S there, of course, alive to all our senses. You can touch it, see it, smell it. But most of all, you can feel it. Yes, New Brighton exists in the present and promises much for the future. But it also lies among the pictures of the mind, where memories link arms with ghosts to stroll along the prom.

It makes you smile and shake your head, whatever your age. You can smell the vinegar on the chips and you can see the little girl with candy-floss on her lips. The wind whips sand from the shore and you can hear the swell of the Wurlitzer organ, the screech of the bickering gulls and the slap of sandals down the pier.

This is New Brighton. But it symbolises all the English seaside resorts, where grand hotels overlook bucket-and-spade shops and you're not sure whether it is now or then. To be sure, we're a little too romantic about it. But why not, it's ours.

Do you know of another place that could afford to lose its tower and pier and still be proud to call itself a resort?

In 1830, James Atherton, a Liverpool builder, thought that Merseyside needed a resort to match the grandeur of old Brighton on the Sussex coast. He bought 170 acres of sandhills and heathland on which he planned his dream. He invited investors to join him in an enterprise, needing £12,000 to build a hotel and ferry. The money was raised in shares worth £100 each. New Brighton became a resort, famed for its hard and clean sands.

By the end of the century, it was rivalling Blackpool, which had built a tower 518ft high. Three years later New Brighton had a tower of 567ft, billed as Britain's answer to the Eiffel Tower in Paris (984ft). ➤

Photographer Colin Lane captured
this spectacular aerial view of The River
Mersey in 2011, showing New Brighton
and Fort Perch Rock with the lighthouse

An aerial shot of
New Brighton
taken in 1976

➤ Such was the confidence of the New Brighton Tower and Recreation Company that they began poaching fine footballers for their own team, New Brighton Tower FC, which played on the nearby athletic ground, sometimes attracting 10,000 spectators. In 1897/98 they entered the Lancashire League, gaining promotion into the second division of the Football League the following season.

However, before the 1901/02 season, the directors closed the club. Although reasonably successful on the field, it had not made enough money to satisfy their appetites. This set an unhappy precedent.

In 1919 the tower was demolished, amid rumours that it was unsafe. Its metal was sold to scrapdealers.

In 1868 the pleasure pier, 550ft long and 70ft wide, was opened. It was rebuilt in 1931 and demolished after a public inquiry in 1978. Seven years earlier the

ferry service from Liverpool had stopped because of silting in the river.

Fort Perch Rock was built in the late 1820s as part of our coastal defences, taking its name from the old navigational lights secured to wooden structures perched on the rock. These days it has museums about Elvis and Merseybeat, a collection of wartime memorabilia and posters and postcards featuring old New Brighton that are a reminder of the old days.

Across the way from the Fort, the newly re-vamped waterfront is taking shape and once again there is a seafront landscape we can be proud of.

New Brighton, beloved of our yesterdays, also has a promising tomorrow.

The new look that will make Brighton rock once again.

"New Brighton symbolises all the
great English seaside resorts"

HAT'S ENTERTAINMENT
Two sharply dressed gents admire the view over the Mersey. Below, paddling in the water makes these children feel as if they're a million miles from the city

SUN AND SAND

Every summer, during the heyday of the
English seaside holiday, thousands of people
would travel to the 'playground of the north'

RED NOSE DAY

Above: Only two things give it away – the hats and the glimpse of the top of
New Brighton Tower. For this is a photograph of the Red Noses, New Brighton,
taken in 1897. The walls were covered with names, and in one was a gate
padlocked and rusting away, with a passageway leading deep into the rock.
Tradition has it that the passages were used to store stolen or smuggled goods

ALL ROADS LEAD
TO NEW BRIGHTON
Below: Harrison Drive in 1939

FOOD FOR THOUGHT

The infamous Ham and Egg parade, a road filled with guesthouses where breakfasts were served in the ground-floor cafes. The road was eventually demolished due to its scandalous reputation because of the illicit activities in the bedrooms upstairs.

THE OLD HAM AND EGG PARADE, NEW BRIGHTON

"New Brighton became a resort, famed for its hard and clean sands. By the end of the century it was rivalling Blackpool."

SADDLE UP

"Each year our family engaged rooms at the seaside where there rows and rows of bathing vans. We would undress in these and horses would take us to the water"

PICTURE THIS
Penny photos on the beach

DONKEY DERBY
What better way to end a day at the seaside than with a donkey ride?

SMUGGLERS' TALES

STORYTELLER Cathy Roberts regales one of her favourite tales about a very unusual New Brighton legendary figure.

All ye that are weary come in an take rest,
Our eggs and our ham they are of the best,
Our ale and our porter are likewise the same,
Step in if you please and give 'em a name.
Mother Redcap.

THIS homely welcome – written on a sign that showed an old woman with a frying pan – gave little to suggest the primary business of the house on the Promenade Walk that became known as 'Mother Redcap's.'

The house itself is now demolished – with a nursing home called Redcap's in its place – but the legend has never diminished. Stories of smugglers, shipwrecks and swashbuckling privateers stretch back through the centuries like the labyrinth of tunnels sitting within the sandstone.

Ostensibly a tavern on the Mersey shore, the house was run by an old lady who always wore a red bonnet . . . Mother Redcap . . . who was known to have the confidence of the many mariners who took advantage of the anchorage – Red bets – near the house.

The thick walls of the house – almost three feet –

provided secure storage for the earnings of sailors, smugglers or privateers, while they were away at sea.

The oak front door was said to have been five inches thick, with a trap door just inside it – possibly intended for over inquisitive customs officials.

At the rear of the house was a dry well that concealed what appeared to be a tunnel entrance – possibly a tunnel that connected to St Hilary's Church, and further into New Brighton.

Many tales have been told in later years of builders uncovering strange recesses, some blocked up with old bottles.

Suggestions of lost fortunes, stashed away in the sandstone 'vaults', would surface, like shells after a tide, only to be submerged again with unsuccessful searching.

Mother Redcap lives on . . .

The old building on the Sandon Promenade at New Brighton, known as Mother Redcap's. Picture taken in 1965 by Bob Bird

GOING UNDERGROUND

Norman Kingham shows a party of youngsters around the underground smugglers' caves at the Yellow Noses, which form part of the garden in Wellington Road. The boys are Ian and David Stuart, Paul and Timothy Kingham, Clive Williams and Peter Haswell.

Below, part of the Wallasey caves thought to have been connected at one time with Mother Redcap's, the reputed haunt of refugees from the press gangs. Pictures taken by Medley / Bird in the 1960s

KING OF THE CASTLE

Simple pleasures – the trusty tools of the bucket and spade, in this photo taken on the sands near Perch Rock in 1987. Opposite page, basking in the sunshine. Photos by Bob Bird

HOLIDAYS IN THE SUN

KEN ROGERS takes a personal journey back in time to Wirral's very own Magic Kingdom.

NEW Brighton was the greatest seaside resort in the whole universe. At least, it was in my mind when I was a kid growing up in the Fifties.

These days, parents all over the world aspire to take their children to places like Walt Disney World Florida or Universal Studios Los Angeles to give them the ultimate theme park experience.

These trips not only knock a hole in your bank balance as big as the Jumbo Jet you will fly in, but also test your patience and staying power to the absolute limit in the wake of several mind-numbing hours in an airport transit lounge before you eventually jet across an ocean with the kids getting increasingly hyper by the hour before Mickey can eventually greet them on the other side of the world.

In post war Liverpool, we journeyed to our local funfair paradise in a matter of minutes, sailing on a Mersey Ferry for the princely sum of a few old pennies. The journey was an incredible experience in its own right. It was actually cheaper to sail to Seacombe and walk the length of the Promenade, giving you a few more precious coins to fulfil your fairground fantasies.

Of course, New Brighton had its own pier then, and thousands of Merseysiders would pile off boat after boat to stride straight into their very own magic kingdom, set out across a gently sloping hill on the river's edge that was crowned with a giant Ballroom, featuring a Tower that rocketed even higher than its world famous counterpart in Blackpool. ➤

Youngsters from Lark Lane in Liverpool take to the water at New Brighton – pictured are Joyce McCassey, Diane Lewis, Susan Fraser, Janet Lewis and Bernadette Bretland in 1971. Picture by Bob Bird

ON THE PROM

An early morning scene on the promenade in 1969

➤ Can you remember the tingling sense of high excitement as the chains of the landing stage bridge rattled out a cast iron song of seaside welcome, dropping a drawbridge to paradise across the heaving decks of ferries like Royal Iris or the Royal Daffodil? The crews desperately tried to hold us back behind the brass marker lines inlaid into the decks. To step an inch over that line invited a crushing trip to the nearest hospital, and so we all took no chances.

We stood at least two inches back, urged by Ferrymen in navy blue sweaters to hold our ground, like the runners and riders at the start of the Grand National. Bang! When that 12 foot high bridge hit the deck, it was the equivalent of the tape going up at Aintree. We now all ran as if our lives depended on it, rushing up the narrow gangway with the fairground sights, sounds and smells urging us to turn our canter into a gallop.

MORNING SUNLIGHT
Taken from the roof of Fort Perch Rock in July 1974. In the distance can be seen the chimeys of Clarence Dock power station and the tower of Liverpool Cathedral

There were now three optional decisions to make. Turn left and rush down the slipway onto the beach to set up camp for the day. This option had the added incentive of an early donkey ride or even a swim in the royal blue Mersey (sewage at no extra charge in those days before United Utilities decided it might be a good idea to clean up the river and invite the fish back!).

Option two was to turn right along the prom towards the spectacular outdoor swimming lido, a giant circular pool where you could sunbathe for England on its terraces (it was always sunny and warm in those days, wasn't it?)

Option three was a straight dash into the fairground and Pleasure Gardens. It was usually parents to the deckchairs on the beach, kids into funfair paradise, a separation that would only be ended by the tempting lunchtime thought of Spam, egg or jam butties, washed down with a bottle of water!

I can still visualise the Fairground. As you entered, ➤

JOY RIDE
Five-year-old Steve Hanrahan leads the field in the 1970s

GIMME SHELTER

Room for a little one? The answer was obviously 'No' on the prom at New Brighton during a heavy thunderstorm in August 1958. Top, the magic of the funfair at the Tower, with the fabulous Figure of 8 rollercoaster ride. Pictures by Medley/Bird

the opportunity to catch a plastic duck on the end of a fishing line was your first temptation. The lads, of course, were instinctively drawn to the most spectacular ride in the park, the giant Figure of 8 rollercoaster ride, with its wooden slats providing a rattling and terrifying thrill of a lifetime. This also gave you a spectacular view of the Tower and Ballroom atop the hill, and the children's amusement park and promenade miniature railway alongside the promenade below.

In previous decades, historic attractions at New Brighton had included the 1910 Aeroplane Ride, a roundabout featuring three large wooden planes that took to the air on the end of crane-like arms. Each plane could hold about six people.

The Caterpillar ride was introduced in the 1940s, circling up and down, each unit attached and painted to resemble the body of a giant caterpillar. This ride sustained itself for generations.

An eggstravaganza of holiday-makers
during the Easter break of 1959

The oldest roundabout in the fairground was said to be the "Dobby Horses" from the 1800s which we called "Bobby Horses", our very own fantasy Grand National.

Old photographs show a Big Wheel as early as 1848, a wooden structure just 30 feet high with about ten double seats. Of course, this would be overshadowed by a later version.

There were Go-Karts by the Boating Lake at the top end of the site, and by 1961 a Cable Car took people from the beach entrance to the upper reaches. I seem to recall two people stood up in each metal 'Car', a tight fit that added to the excitement and danger. There were side stalls all across the site. My favourite was the Donkey Derby where you rolled a wooden ball towards a series of holes. Hitting those furthest away would gallop your horse quicker across the horizontal track, as the 'commentator 'whipped up the excitement. I can remember winning a kite which I later flew on the beach for hours on end.

At the end of the day, exhausted, but supremely ➤

LIFE'S A BEACH

While Mersey shipping was dodging the fog banks, crowds on the beach at nearby Egremont were sunbathing on the last day of the school holidays in 1961

FAIRY TAIL
One for the family album, as these
youngsters saddle up on the beach in 1955

happy, we would have to trek along the prom to the Seacombe landing stage for the 'cheaper' ferry journey back across the river, having spent almost every penny in our riverside paradise. We would then have to walk home from the Pier Head to our inner city Liverpool streets.

I felt privileged that at night I could see the coloured lights of New Brighton from where I lived on Everton's famous ridge, one of the highest vantage points in the city. I could also see the ferry boats from up there, plying their trade on a daily basis. Those fairground lights would twinkle and send out a tantalising "come back soon" message that none of us could resist.

I also have a huge pride in the fact that the New Brighton resort was fashioned in the mind of one of my personal heroes, James Atherton, the merchant who in 1815 built Everton's historic St George's – the Cast Iron Church – where I would sing in the choir in the Fifties. ➤

The allure of the Cafe de Paris for a time-old tea ritual

An ideal stop for a picnic in 1966.
Picture by Bob Bird

➤ Atherton built many mansions in the district, and his own stood to the left of the west gate of St George's with his garden stretching down from Northumberland Terrace to Netherfield Road.

This gave him an uninterrupted view of the River Mersey at that time, and he was continually fascinated by a strip of land on the Wirral side that was known as "Black Rock."

In 1830, Atherton, in association with his son-in-law William Rowson, began negotiations with John Penkett, Lord of the Manor of Liscard, to purchase this land at the north-eastern end of the Township.

Effectively, his successful development of Everton represented a blueprint for his subsequent plans for New Brighton.

Atherton had proved to be an astute businessman

The best seat in the house? Picture by Medley & Bird

Palace of dreams – crowds line the promenade to admire the view in 1958. Picture by Bob Bird

with an eye for profit and he recognised the enormous seaside potential of "Black Rock" both as a resort, and for the building of further smart mansions for the rich.

He also recognised that his own Everton mansion would soon be over-run by thousands of back to back terraced streets that were encroaching up the hill from the dock gates. This precipitated his move to New Brighton.

On January 24, 1832, William Rowson advanced a deposit of £200 to John Penkett to buy the "New Brighton Estate". The sum represented £100 each for himself and James Atherton.

This £200 would become the "deposit" for the seaside resort that would eventually capture the imagination of hundreds of thousands of Merseysiders and shape our childhood leisure days so magnificently, giving Liverpool families crucial respite from poverty and two World Wars.

James Atherton died in 1838. His dream would inspire us all for well over a century and we should thank him for the magic kingdom of New Brighton and a thousand childhood memories that we will never forget.

Flying high – this picture by Stephen Shakeshaft captures the view from the chairlift to the fairground in 1966

Wish You Were Here . . . !

Promenade. Egremont.

IN 1974, Paul Holliday spotted a solitary postcard in the window of a small antique shop in Victoria Road.

The discovery left its mark on him and it was the start of a collection that is really something to write home about. He now owns over 120 postcards whose images reflect an elegant and genteel age that has long since disappeared.

Paul, General Manager of the Floral Pavilion, says: "The postcards are really a history of the town. The appeal to me was that I was and always will be fascinated by New Brighton's rise and fall and now, of course, its rise again.

"That first one cost about 50p – which doesn't sound a lot but, at the time, it certainly was. I eventually bought quite a few from the shop in Victoria Road – ironically the last one I bought was at an antique and collectors' fair held at the Floral Pavilion in 2010 and which cost me £8.

"My favourite is one showing the bandstand in Victoria Gardens which is now exactly where the stage of the new Floral is. When the theatre was being rebuilt I was based at the Pacific Road Arts Centre in Birkenhead and during that time my postcard album went missing. I was absolutely devastated."

Luckily for Paul it was a case of 'Return to Sender'…

"Just a few months ago it re-surfaced in a storeroom cupboard," he explains. "Now my postcards are really back home."

ROYAL FERRY HOTEL, VICTORIA ROAD, NEW BRIGHTON.

New Brighton Tower.

THE PROMENADE, NEW BRIGHTON.

THE PIER, NEW BRIGHTON.

221000

Uncle Joe, THE NEW BRIGHTON CHILDREN'S FAVOURITE ENTERTAINER

Tower and Gardens, New Brighton.

BOATING POOL AND PROMENADE, NEW BRIGHTON.

Children's Corner, showing Battery, New Brighton

BANDSTAND AND PAVILION, NEW BRIGHTON PIER.

209356.

21029

New Brighton. The Landing Stage.

Vale Park, New Brighton.

Lighthouse, New Brighton.

BOATING LAKE, TOWER GROUNDS, NEW BRIGHTON.

G 7080.

New Brighton from the Fort

SHORE & RED NOSES, NEW BRIGHTON.

THE FORT, NEW BRIGHTON.

FUN AND GAMES
Crowds enjoy a scorcher at
New Brighton Pool in August 1938

BATHING BELLES

WHEN Merseyside's favourite open air swimming pools were making waves.

CROWDS flocked to the new Derby Bathing Pool in Wallasey when it was opened in 1932.

The Liverpool ECHO reported: "Wallasey's £50,000 new bathing pool is certainly drawing the crowds and the shore is invaded on sunny Sundays by thousands who come by ferry, bus, tram and train.

"The popularity of the new pool is amazing; policemen are needed to control the queues."

Later that year, plans started for an even bigger pool. New Brighton Pool was opened by Lord Leverhulme on June 3, 1934. At a cost of £90,000 it was the largest lido in Britain. Its magnificent art deco styling made it a design classic and bathers loved the contoured shallows and high diving boards. In 1937 the pool celebrated its millionth visitor, Mary Drew, who had travelled from Coventry. Over the years the venue played host to wrestling competitions, midnight bathing, dances and the Miss New Brighton contest.

In 1984, ITV staged a spectacular outdoor concert at the pool. 'New Brighton Rock' starred Nik Kershaw, Frankie Goes to Hollywood, Spandau Ballet, the Weather Girls and the Royal Liverpool Philharmonic Orchestra in a four-day musical extravaganza.

But, in the late 1980s the crowds at the pool dwindled. Holiday-makers were travelling abroad for the summers and New Brighton Pool, like so many around the country, suffered from a lack of investment. When storms damaged the structure of the pool, the council decided that it was too expensive to repair. In 1990 it was demolished.

LUCKY DIP

Above: The Derby Swimming Pool at Harrison Drive removed any tedious waiting for tide-time to have an exhilirating dip in 1932. For those who didn't have a queue jumping baths contract, the wire fence offered a sneaky way of getting in quicker – and for free

Right: Floodlit bathing at New Brighton Pool in 1947 – during a warm spell in August the pool was open until 11pm

CHUTE TO THRILL

The water slide proves an irresistible
attraction in June 1947

MAKING WAVES

New Brighton Pool was opened by Lord Leverhulme in 1934 and was the largest lido in Britain. The main picture shows spectators elbow to elbow in 1955 and inset, some daring divers take the plunge in 1983

The judges seem a little over-dressed compared to the ladies, in this Bob Bird photograph from August 1983

STAR ATTRACTION

FROM Hollywood stars to homegrown talent, New Brighton was the backdrop to a world of glitz and glamour.

IN the days when New Brighton was a place for classy functions, live broadcasts, big dances, celebrity concerts and other engagements, many films stars went there.

Stewart Granger, Susan Hayward and Robert Beatty were among them. The town even played host to American bombshell Mae West when she re-opened the town's popular Grand Hotel. Built on the seafront, the hotel was one of the most glamorous for holidaymakers in the area.

New Brighton had its own homegrown glamour too as the 1950s and 1960s were the heyday of seaside beauty contests. The Miss New Brighton competition started in 1949 and was held at the open air swimming pool. Up to 15,000 people were reported to have watched the Final in 1949 and over the next two decades the competition went from strength to strength. Edna MacFarlane scooped the first ever Miss New Brighton title in 1949 and the 1950 winner Violet Pretty went on to become the famous film actress Anne Heywood.

IT'S A GRAND LIFE
Movie star Mae West at the opening of The Grand Hotel

Joan Boardman, Wirral's first Miss New Brighton winner in 1959, said she was "petrified" at what her mum would say when she entered the competition. Joan from Wallasey was 20 when she took part in

LUCKY SEVEN

Ready for the final parade – the sun was hot when seven of the Miss New Brighton competitors took an early stroll at the pool before the contest in 1968

CHEEKY CHARM

A kiss from Merseybeat singer Billy J Kramer for 20-year-old Rosslyn Tranfield of New Brighton at the poolside beauty pageant in July 1978

the event, after being encouraged to enter by the local photographer Bob Bird. At her first attempt she came second but this turned out to be her springboard to success as she went on to become Miss England and was sixth in the Miss Universe competition. But the Miss New Brighton title was the one she wanted and Joan returned a year later to become the first local winner.

Many people will recall the resort's open air pool packed with spectators watching hopefuls parade.

There were weekly heats, watched by huge crowds and often judged by famous entertainers. But by the 1980s many of the competitions across the country were being stopped and New Brighton's last major competition was in 1989.

LET'S HEAR IT FOR THE BOYS!

Above: Wallasey beach patrolmen muscle in on the action in 1967 – front row, Bernard Brabin, David Martin, Martyn Riley and John Hopkins. Back row, Bob Ruddell, David Meyer, Norman Thompson, Don Malcolmson, Ian Muat, Rex Bird, Pete Ruddell. Picture by Bob Bird.

Right: Fire Service personnel taking exercise at the Derby Swimming Pool in 1944, which the Wallasey Council loaned to the service as a fitness training camp

POOL OF TALENT

Above: New Brighton Baths as 9,000 watch the joint attraction of the ASA diving competition and the heats of the Miss New Brighton competition.
Picture by Bob Bird

"Many will recall the resort's open air pool packed with spectators watching the hopefuls parade"

RISING STARS

Budding Beauty Queens, Joanne Burke, Tamsin O'Hanlon and Amanda Rickerby in June 1979. Picture by Medley & Bird

BEATLEMANIA HITS THE BALLROOM

PROMOTER Sam Leach reflects on his life-long love affair with a world famous venue.

THE Tower Ballroom was my favourite place to promote bands – and The Beatles loved it, too.

I know – I was there. Lennon loved it. I believe it helped put The Beatles on the map.

Years before I had danced there to the sounds of the Joe Loss' Big Band. Little did I know that one day I would promote the best band of all time there.

I recall a miserable day in October 1961, when I took the ferry boat ride to New Brighton and got drenched, yet I excitedly stood in the rain knowing I was sailing towards my destiny – Operation Big Beat starring The Beatles.

Bill Roberts and Tom McCardle, the Tower directors, didn't initially share my enthusiasm but decided to give me a chance. When I said we'd break the attendance record they laughed uproariously.

"You'll never beat Joe Loss, Sam," they said together.

A week later I returned with the tickets and posters. Tom shouted: "Sam, the phone hasn't stopped. We said it would be BIG . . . didn't we?"

I suppressed a laugh. Big was an understatement.

My first two promotions on November 10 and 24, 1961, drew 4,100 and 4,600 respectively, not only beating the Tower's own records, but the Beatles' own mainland records as well.

Even better, they were acclaimed as the "most exciting shows in Merseybeat history" by top music critics.

Financially speaking, I made two years average wages on each show. Oh, yes, I loved the Tower.

In previous years it had been a bit of a 'white

elephant' and the lovely little seaside resort had almost become a ghost town.

I am proud of the fact that with a little help from my friends – The Beatles, Gerry and The Pacemakers, Rory Storm and the Hurricanes, Kingsize Taylor and the Dominos and The Remo Four, we gave it a much-needed kiss of life.

I still love this unique little town that will always be a part of me.

Looking back if The Tower hadn't burned down, I'd have still been promoting there.

I was the only one who made it pay, mainly because I ran a late transport network with Wallasey's local businesses, who gave me bottles of champagne when I decided to quit the Tower, as a touching 'thank you' for bringing them so much trade.

Today Merseybeat still lives on courtesy of the Fort Perch Rock, which houses a Merseybeat Hall of Fame in which I was the first 'inductee'. I am so proud of that.

New Brighton … my kind of town.

HARD TO BEAT

Posters from the Leach Entertainments' events at the Tower Ballroom, featuring The Beatles and a host of Merseybeat stars. Opposite page, a Beatles performance from the early days with Pete Best on drums. Below, John Lennon and Ringo Starr rock the Tower Ballroom

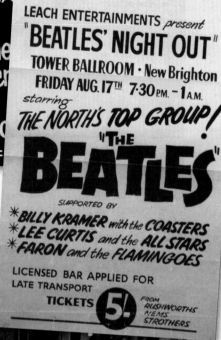

ROCK AND ROLLING

The Rolling Stones played at the Tower Ballroom on August 10, 1964, as part of the Rael-Brook/Cavern Club Beat Group contest. In his book 'Stone Alone', Bill Wyman says: "Elaborate plans had been made to get us into the venue by means of a chair-lift, but it was finally decided that it would be too dangerous if fans got out of hand. The crowd of 5,000 got out of hand anyway. We waited five hours to go on stage and, despite some laughs backstage with Jimmy Saville, one of the contest judges, we were already tired. Fighting began when we struck up the music; it was Mods versus Rockers, with the Tower Ballroom's spotlights picking out the fights! The battle lasted 45 minutes and 50 youths had been ejected from the hall, two with knives. We had orders to carry on as normal, and so we played a set of fourteen songs and there was no arrests."

TOWER OF TALENT

Above, the crowd at the Rolling Stones concert at the Tower Ballroom in 1964.
Below, the ballroom towers over the funfair and beach in this photograph by G Mayson

FLORAL STILL BLOOMING WITH AN ALL-STAR CAST

PAUL HOLLIDAY, Manager of the Floral Pavilion, shares his memories of New Brighton

THE 'Floral' has of course been such an important part of my life – little did I know when I first performed there all those years ago, that I'd one day become manager and see the whole theatre transformed into the jewel in the crown it is today.

When I first joined the Floral Pavilion as Assistant Manager back in 1974 it still had a twice-nightly Summer Season show – 6.30 and 8.45 Monday to Saturday – and in a 1000-seat theatre an awful lot of seats to fill! So many stars have appeared at the Floral and it has been my pleasure to see so many of them over the years. Like Hollywood legend Howard Keel, fantastic singers like Vic Damone and Jack Jones as well of course as our own 'home grown' stars like Norman Wisdom, Petula Clark, Frankie Howerd . . . the list goes on and on.

As a young boy growing up in the 1950s I have the happiest of memories of New Brighton. The school summer holidays that seemed to go on forever, particularly, walking along the promenade from Seacombe, past Egremont and its beach with soft golden sand, then carrying on past old Mother Redcap's cottage with its dark and scary tales of smuggling and piracy on the North Wirral coastline.

Along past Vale Park with its traditional bandstand and rows and rows of deckchairs where, for six weeks every summer, 'Joytime' childrens show, compered by Uncle Norman and Aunty Dorothy would be held every day, and then there were relaxing brass band concerts on Sunday afternoons. Further along was Tommy Mann's miniature railway which took you through a magical grotto where it stopped for a few moments to marvel at a small funfair scene.

HORSING AROUND

Frank Carson serves panto pony Spangles after a show at the Floral Pavilion in January 1984

The Floral Pavilion, pictured in July 1962

Organist Lesly Haskell goes through a number with Mavis White and Peggy Naylor in 1968. Picture by Bob Bird

Of course, dominating the whole of the area was the enormous New Brighton Tower, no longer with its original tower – which had been taken down during the First World War – but a huge theatre and ballroom complex. The cable car took you on a perilous journey from ground level right up to the top of the Tower building. The view was spectacular, you'd look down at the crowded promenade and beach teeming with day trippers who'd arrived by every conceivable form of transport. You could also see the roof of the famous Tivoli Theatre and the pleasure pier and landing stage.

Victoria Road was the main thoroughfare and was packed with cafes, bingo parlours, gift shops and a Woolworth's store. There were also two cinemas, the Court and the Trocadero.

Further along the prom was (and of course still is) the indoor funfair, at one time the largest of its kind, and opposite was Marine Lake with its small rowing boats and a larger motor boat that was able to take family groups round the lake for sixpence . . .

"All aboard the Skylark!"

During the Summer I assisted in staging the 'Miss New Brighton Bathing Beauty Contest' and 'New Brighton Rosebud Contest' at the open air bathing pool. I also performed at the Floral Pavilion in the early Sixties, singing and dancing with a local dance school, and then as a member of Wallasey Operatic Society on many occasions.

Since reopening in 2008 the Floral is now well on the way to becoming a major touring theatre venue with West End musicals such as 'Cabaret', 'Annie' and later this year the fantastic 'Blood Brothers'. Drama productions have really taken off as well,

with the Agatha Christie thrillers 'Witness for the Prosecution' and 'Verdict' and the comedy 'Stepping Out'.

As the new 'Marine Point' development takes shape on the site of the old bathing Pool its clear that the renaissance of New Brighton has begun in earnest – and long may it continue to do so.

MEMORIES OF A LIDO LOVELY

MAUREEN WALSH, BBC broadcaster, recalls a golden era of treading the boards

THE Pier and Floral Pavilion Theatre during the Fifties hold so many memories for me.

One of my most romantic moments was catching the late ferry after dancing in the Tower Ballroom to Bill Gregson's Band. I was 16 at the time and only allowed to go if my older cousin, Jacqueline, took me. I was dance mad – I'd go anywhere just as long as I could dance.

One particular Saturday evening, on the last ferry from New Brighton to Liverpool, the singer Eric Bentley started chatting to us and took a 'shine' to me.

We stood at the bows of the ferry and he sang to me 'Stay As Sweet As You Are' – you could say that was my 'Titanic' moment!

Being one of Jackson Earle's Lido Lovelies in my first Summer Season at the Floral Pavilion Theatre was a great training ground for hard work. In the 1950s New Brighton was buzzing with lots of visitors all enjoying their two weeks holiday.

To ensure they saw a different show each week throughout the summer season, Joy Caville, the choreographer, taught us six routines for six different shows.

That was 36 routines and 36 costumes, each one especially made for us by a lady called Peggy.

We were at the theatre for 10 in the morning to rehearse the show we would perform the following week.

Those rehearsals would continue until lunchtime

BEST SEAT IN THE HOUSE

Above, the Floral Pavilion Theatre Group in 1974. Picture by Bob
Bird. Opposite page, visiting from London, Connie Parker and
Angela Shinn take refuge from the crowds in the Floral Pavilion
gardens in August 1957. Below, a poster for the Victoria Gardens
and Pavilion, another wonderful New Brighton theatre

VICTORIA GARDENS
AND
PAVILION,
NEW BRIGHTON.

GENERAL MANAGER.........MR. HOWARD INNES.

ENORMOUS ATTRACTIONS,
OPENING NIGHT,
MONDAY, MAY 5TH,
and Daily 2-30 o'clock and 7-30 p.m.

THE MERSEY ENTERTAINERS;—
THE MYSTERIOUS VIOLAS.
DOROTHY WELSH.
DOUGLAS STUART.
ALBERT MAIDEN.
GRETA WRAY.
HOWARD INNES.
JACK HYLTON.
PROF. NORTON,
and
The VICTORIA BIJOU ORCHESTRA.

PRICES—3d., 6d., and 1s.

when we would eat and prepare for a matinee
performance at half two.

We would go on to perform, what we called
'two houses', a show at half six and then another
at half eight.

No wonder the dancers were always hungry.

We couldn't afford to eat in the Theatre Café so
I had the bright idea of turning the electric fire
(our only form of heating in the dressing room)
onto it's back and buying a whistling kettle to
make our hot drinks. I know!

Could you imagine health and safety officers
accepting that these days?

During one performance we forgot to take the
whistling kettle off the heat. The scene at the
time was supposedly Ireland and the Priest was
giving advice to the villagers when the kettle
came to the boil. Promises were made not to use
the kettle again – but we did.

The dancers dressing room was beneath the
stage and when there was a high tide somehow
the dressing room flooded. There were a few
occasions when we had to iron our costumes dry.

But we were happy, we were healthy and
always smiling. I'm smiling now just thinking of
those wonderful days.

The following text appears on the poster within the image:

TIVOLI
THEATRE
NEW BRIGHTON.

Director of Entertainments .... Mr. FRED WILLMOT.
Manager .... Mr. F. V. ROSS.

6-50 | TWICE NIGHTLY | 9

The Greatest Vaudeville Co. ever presented to the Public OF WALLASEY.

ALL STAR HOLIDAY PROGRAMME.

MONDAY, December 28, 1914
AND DURING THE WEEK.

THE ONLY THEATRE IN THE BOROUGH PLAYING HIGH-CLASS VAUDEVILLE.

AT ENORMOUS EXPENSE, THE WORLD'S GREATEST CORNET SOLOIST, MISS

DAISY SQUELCH
AND COMPANY.

BERTRAM BANKS

MATINEE New Year's Day at 2-30

RAITON & RICHE

E. M. SPATE THE GREAT CANADIAN BARITONE.

BRET HAYDEN, Whistler and Mimic.

THE NIPPERS

THE TIVOLIOSCOPE WILL PRESENT THE LATEST PATHE GAZETTE.

THE THREE BUCKLEYS

NEXT WEEK: **BABES IN THE WOOD**

STARS OF THE DAY

The Tivoli Theatre opened in 1914 and was very popular in its heyday, presenting variety shows, plays and films.
The theatre closed in 1955 and the building later became an amusement arcade

Happy holidaymakers throng the sands at Perch Rock in August 1951.

ROCK OF AGES

PETER GRANT on the coastal battery fort that is still gunning for glory.

IT is one of Wirral's best-known landmarks and the cornerstone of the peninsula.

Built as a coastal battery fort, between 1825 and 1829, to protect the Port of Liverpool against a perceived Napoleonic threat to Britain, it has kept watch over the entrance to the River Mersey ever since.

Today Fort Perch Rock contrasts architecturally with the new multi-million pound development on the site of the former New Brighton swimming pool.

The Fort is owned by the wonderful Darroch family, who run it as a museum and a fascinating place to visit. With the nearby New Brighton lighthouse, it is easily found being located opposite the new Floral Pavilion theatre.

Curator Doug Darroch says there is much to see

within those red sandstone walls that came from a quarry at Runcorn and were floated down the Mersey during construction.

Doug says: "It is approached by a causeway and entered through an impressive archway above which has a Coat of Arms. Once inside, you are in a courtyard surrounded by a sense of history and faced with the dilemma of where to explore first."

A cannon to the left, cannon to the right and cannon to the front. A cannon still volleys and thunders to welcome passing ocean cruise liners, or to salute warships on a goodwill visit. The fort's guns have only been fired twice as a wartime action in its entire history. Dougie and enthusiastic volunteer helpers are continually adding exhibits to keep the museum alive with things to see. ➤

Visitors to Perch Rock
in 1938

"Built as a coastal battery fort to protect the Port of Liverpool it has kept watch over the entrance to the River Mersey ever since."

➤ Says Doug: "The displays of wreckage of WW2 aircraft and the Spitfire fighter that crashed in Birkenhead Park are permanent and popular features. Each aeronautical object, large or small, has a story to tell. The fort is packed with stories."

Liverpool's naval past and Birkenhead's ship building heritage are told in a large room housing a huge model of the Cammell Laird built HMS Prince of Wales.

The Prince of Wales was Britain's newest battleship in WW2 and took part in the fateful engagement with German battleship Bismarck as told in the film 'Sink the Bismarck'.

The Prince of Wales was later sunk by Japanese aircraft with heavy loss of life.

The model at Fort Perch Rock is to be admired for its detail and size as it can be sailed by a man sitting inside the superstructure.

Says Doug: "The story of submarine HMS Thetis that sank in Liverpool Bay and the subsequent rescue attempts is told in period newspaper cuttings and photographs from 1939. A few steps lead to the walls that offer spectacular views of the Mersey Estuary.

"Here is housed an exhibition devoted to the history of 610 Squadron (County of Chester) that was originally based at Hooton Park but moved to Biggin Hill to take part in the Battle of Britain."

A walk around the walls offers contrasting views, North, South, East and West and where the guns once stood is apparent. From these fortifications, the first shots of World War I were fired to warn a Norwegian sailing ship – that ignored wartime restrictions – making its approach. A second shot hit the bow of a liner at anchor.

In World War II the Fort Perch Rock Battery again fired the first British shots, just 15 minutes after Prime Minister Neville Chamberlain declared war on Germany on September 3, 1939.

A fishing boat had entered the restricted Rock Channel and the fort fired a warning shot across its bow.

Says Doug: "The whole of Fort Perch Rock is steeped in history, all 4,000 square yards ➤

Fort Perch Rock curator, Doug Darroch

➤ and to think that this unique building was built a few pence under budget for £26,965 and eight old pence!"

The fort was 'dismantled' as a military establishment in the early 1950s after ceremonially firing its guns during the Festival of Britain.

During WW2 it was equipped with radar and today it houses a modern, high tech radar station.

After being decommissioned, the fort was sold at auction to funfair owner Tommy Mann and his business partner Tommy Kershaw. In 1976 local architect Norman Kingham became the owner/custodian, followed by Doug Darroch, father of the present curator Doug Darroch.

Lovers of the Merseybeat scene of the 1960s will find many photographs of Beat groups of that era in the Merseybeat Gallery, where talks on the subject are regularly staged on a Sunday.

The fort also stages live outdoor pop concerts during the summer months.

Throughout the year 'Tales Around the Fire' are told in front of a wood burning open fireplace with a topical theme such as 'Dragons seeking Valentines' to celebrate Valentine's Day.

Doug says: "The attraction of Fort Perch Rock is that there is much to see and explore whatever the weather. On a brisk or sunny clear day the views from the walls are both bracing and spectacular

"When it rains, there are many enclosed exhibits plus a café for a drink and bite to eat. Fort Perch Rock also has a licensed bar and can be hired."

The Darroch family came to the Fort in 1976, part of the Warplane Wreck Investigation Group (WWIG). 2011 is the group's 40th year and over the last four decades it has recovered many wrecks of wartime aircraft on Merseyside. The most notable of these is the Spitfire P7533 which was recovered in Birkenhead park in October 2007.

Doug, could you live anywhere else?

"No way!" he says.

WHATEVER THE WEATHER

Opposite page, top to bottom: The time-honoured seaside tradition of a donkey ride at New Brighton in 1945. A poster from the 1970s celebrating 150 years of the Fort Perch Rock. The fury of the Mersey as a storm reaches its peak in 1990

TORCH SONG

By PETER GRANT

I am a lighthouse keeper. . .
The last one around
It's the only job I ever wanted
My feet have never touched the ground
Every day I see the sea
Seagulls are great company
The best part of it all is that I do some good
Even though the teachers said I never would
Each night I hug the moon
and shake hands with stars
I look through my telescope and
wave at Saturn and Mars
I am up in the world and I really do care
That sailors and ships know I'm there
I don't get lonely
I'm very easy to please
I am home now
Don't need any front door keys
Oh this was always the only job you see
At Perch Rock, I sleep soundly,
Just me
 . . . and the sea.

ALL WHITE
ON THE NIGHT

One of New Brighton's more unusual
spring cleaning jobs for Harry Hitchin and
Andy Penkethman, as they repaint the
lighthouse in time for the Queen's Silver
Jubilee visit to Merseyside in 1977

LANDMARK LIGHT

The lighthouse – or the Perch Rock Light as is its full title – remains a prominent landmark at the entrance to the River Mersey. Above, this aerial view in 1934 shows the lighthouse, Fort Perch Rock and Derby Bathing Pool. Below, photographer Colin Lane captures New Brighton from the sky in 2010

A HEAVENLY ESCAPE

EVERY summer, during the heyday of the English seaside holiday, hundreds of thousands of people would travel to the 'Playground of the North'.

FOR the Mersey area particularly, New Brighton was the great escape. It was clean, at the mouth of the river which gave fresh, sea breezes and it was also just a short ferry ride away, a big attraction for the city toiler and day-tripper.

Many visitors to New Brighton and other seaside resorts round Britain would have arrived in comfort by train – possibly sending their luggage ahead. Railway companies produced a range of colourful and eye-catching posters for railway station platforms. They offered passengers an enticing view of holiday destinations when overseas holidays were beyond the financial reach of most.

TICKET TO RIDE

Above, from 1923 until 1948 the Wirral lines of the Mersey Railway were operated by LMS. In 1938 they completed the electrification of the lines on Wirral. This picture shows one of the early electric trains arriving at New Brighton. Opposite page, bright sunshine but low temperatures meant that overcoats were the order of the day for these ferry passengers in the Fifties

ADVENTURE OF A LIFETIME

MEMORIES of that first trip to New Brighton will be with historian Frank Carlyle forever.

WHEN I was five or six, my Aunty Leah said to me: "I'm taking you to New Brighton on a boat tomorrow, Francis."

New Brighton...and on a boat! Where's that? It could have been anywhere on the planet. This was going to be a great adventure for me - I'd never even heard of this 'New Brighton'. My Aunty had only recently married 'Uncle Gerry,' so they decided to give me a day out. I remember going on a tram down to the Pier Head. It was chocca – everybody seemed to be going to New Brighton on that sunny day. I'd never seen such huge crowds before and it was a little frightening, but I knew I was safe because it was me who gripped my Aunty and Uncle's hands even tighter.

This was going to be my very first ever ride on the ferry. When it was time to go down the floating bridge to catch the boat, I loosened my grip and had the most exhilarating run in my entire life.

Standing with 'millions' like me, waiting to board, was well worth the wait. I could smell the salt air, feel the warm breeze, hear all the noises – the engine, people talking, children shouting – it all added to the excitement. The saltiness of the breeze caught my attention as I stood against the rail. I'd never experienced anything like it. When we finally arrived at New Brighton, people were jostling for position, ready to get off. With hands gripped even tighter, we got off. I remember being allowed to run, on my own, along the prom and past lots of people looking out across the river towards Liverpool.

Suddenly there was loud music, all different types and lovely aromas. The fairground was where I had my first doughnut and I can still taste it now.

SNACK ATTACK

Some tasty seaside treats on offer here – cockles, mussels, oysters, shrimps, crabs, whelks, winkles...not to mention the potato crisps, pies, cakes, teas and delicious ices!

Candy floss was eaten in seconds. Then I turned to face another first – the Helter Skelter. It looked like a huge turret. It was eerily dark. I climbed the spiral staircase with Aunt Leah. There was a man standing at the top. "Don't be afraid," he said as he put me on a mat and gave me a shove

Down and around and down I went until I reached the bottom, where Uncle Gerry was waiting to catch me.

Then we walked along the pier where 'millions' of people talked and ate at the same time. A group of young men and girls were giggling while they had their photos taken. We had our pictures taken next – if only I had one now. That moment is lost in a great dream sequence. But it happened.

It was dinner time – we had chips, that's all anyone seemed to be eating.

Then we went into a building where lots of people were putting pennies into rows of machines. Winners cheered, losers moaned and the mechanical robots clinked and clanked.

"Everybody seemed to be going to New Brighton on that sunny day"

Uncle put pennies into one of them, but nothing came out. Bit like life. Outside, we headed across to the beach, where I was ordered to take off my socks and shoes and paddle. It was great, kicking water at Aunty and Uncle. But they didn't seem to see the funny side and I was told off. It didn't stop me though.

It was time to go home. We walked back to the ferry, with me waving a little Union Jack flag on a stick. It was a wonderful day, coming to a close. As the ferry reached home, I couldn't wait to run over that floating bridge again. But this time I was just walking quickly, to catch the tram back home. I might have lost that photo, but that fantastic day is a memory I'll always treasure, with Aunty Leah, Uncle George, New Brighton and me.

FERRY CROSS THE MERSEY
Holidaymakers depart from the Royal Iris onto the north passenger bridge at New Brighton ferry terminal in 1962

RIVER RESCUERS

ONE of only four Royal National Lifeboat Institute stations that operate an inland rescue hovercraft alongside the conventional lifeboat, the New Brighton lifeboat service has achieved an outstanding record of bravery over the years, with 48 awards for gallantry.

The heart-warming story began in 1851, when Coxswains Peter Cropper, Thomas Evans and Joseph Formby were awarded silver medals for their long service on the Liverpool Dock Trustees Lifeboat.

Twelve years later, the RNLI established a lifeboat station, and a tubular lifeboat was kept on moorings on the river Mersey.

Thomas Evans again received a silver medal, along with his son, Thomas, and William Evans, for rescuing 55 people from a stricken vessel.

In 1893, a steam-powered lifeboat, the Duke of Northumberland, was put into service, followed in 1923 by the first motor life boat, William and Kate Johnston.

In 1954, a motor boarding boat was put into service, donated by Liverpool University Students' Panto Day. The vessel was subsequently called Panto (oh, yes it was).

In 1973 the station became an inshore rescue service, when the all-weather lifeboat was withdrawn.

An Atlantic 21 B Class vessel started operating the following May.

Then, in 1995, an Atlantic 75 B class lifeboat was put into service, named Rocklight after the Lighthouse.

The inshore hovercraft, Hurley Spirit - donated by Mrs. Kay Hurley - was launched in 2005, to enable the crew to reach areas where a conventional lifeboat cannot operate.

The lifeboat continually operates in some of the most challenging conditions, manned entirely by volunteers. 48 awards, but so many more lives saved.

The New Brighton lifeboat makes its way to Princes Stage with the skipper of the Bar lightship Captain Harold Hooton and Dr Thomas Shirkey after they had been marooned on board the lightship for six days in June 1968

The lifeboat Norman B Corlett at Princes Dock during a naming ceremony by the Duchess of Kent in March 1951. The lines of bunting and the watching crowd forms a gala framework to a big moment and the Duchess's visit

Life savers at a parade and inspection at New Brighton in June 1950

A cool-down in the water was just too tempting for this shaggy dog – fortunately PC Peter Smith and beach patrolman Joe Pringle were there to rescue him from the doggy stroke in 1970

Members of the Wallasey Recreations Committee watch the Corporation's new inshore rescue craft undergoing tests in 1967. Patrolmen Peter Ruddell and Tom Caldwell demonstrate the craft but there's just one problem – where does the rescued person sit?

THE BEAUTIFUL GAME

THE brief reign of New Brighton Tower FC, proved you can't always buy success.

THE problem for the money men behind that great tower, standing like a sentinel over the resort, was that if they couldn't find some way of attracting crowds to the shores of the Mersey at New Brighton during the winter, there would be no tomorrows for any of them.

And then someone said a word which electrified them all. "Football" was drawing huge crowds to stadiums all over the country. Across the river,

Everton and Liverpool were doing particularly well. Why shouldn't there be a third big football club on Merseyside? So the New Brighton Tower and Recreation Company decided to buy a football team to play on the athletic ground, already built in the shadow of their huge steel structure of 567ft 6ins. These were men of ambition.

New Brighton Tower FC was formed in 1897 and soon, the club were elected into the Football

New Brighton FC centre forward Johnny Vincent. Picture by Medley / Bird

League Second Division. But the desire was for First Division status. The Towerites went close to reaching the target but success had not come quickly enough for the businessmen and in 1901 they withdrew their support.

It was not until 1921 that the idea of senior football was actively pursued. Based at the Rake Lane ground, the club soon became known as The Rakers. Following a good first season in the Lancashire Combination they were elected to the Football League Third Division (North) during the summer of 1922. Rakers enjoyed membership of the League until 1951 when they failed in the attempts to gain re-election. By that time home matches were being staged at the Tower Grounds, Rake Lane having been damaged during the war and then requisitioned by the local council for housing. After leaving the League and rejoining ➤

the Lancashire Combination, the club nearly folded in 1954.

However, the changing fortunes of football were made obvious to all when just a couple of years later Rakers were making national headlines with a tremendous run in the FA Cup. League and cup successes were commonplace and hopes of returning to the Football League still existed. But by the mid-1960s the world was changing rapidly – the club was unable to compete financially and was finding it increasingly difficult to maintain the vast Tower Grounds.

These pressures became too great and there was a short spell at Coronation Park, in Greasby, before New Brighton left the Cheshire County League and then folded in 1983.

In 1993 a group of local footballers playing for Old Wallaseyans decided to restore the New Brighton name to the football pages. Home fixtures were staged at Harrison Park, where the club are today – a far cry from the previous stadia and those days in the Football League but a club with perhaps more realistic ideas and expectations.

Programme dated Saturday, September 10, 1898, and the line-up for New Brighton Tower FC versus Gainsborough Trin

NEED FOR SPEED

A crowd of 3,000 watched the motorcycle prom racing in 1960

DIFFERENT DRUM

British Stock Car Racing in the 1950s to the 1970s was world famous. New Brighton had its place. New Brighton track was regarded as the "most frightening Oval" in the UK. The track and Oval evolved from a high-banked cycle track, one of the many diverse entertainment facilities at New Brighton, from 1900 onwards. Even old bangers could reach terrifying speeds. It was well constructed – a concrete bowl with steel posts and a cable fence. The picture above shows a Boys' Brigade band leading the Hot Rods around the track before a race in 1972

TEE TIME
Left, Wallasey Golf Club, the new Bayswater Road to Harrison Drive, in March 1938

AN OASIS OF GREEN

VALE PARK was established in 1899 with the purchase, by Wallasey Urban District Council, of the Liscard Vale estate. The aim was to create a 'breathing space' for the increasing population.

THE grounds opened as Vale Park on May 20, 1899.

Vale House is thought to have been built around 1830, possibly as a family home for a Cotton broker.

The Liverpool businessman and local Justice of the Peace, Charles Holland, lived at the property for moe than 50 years. An extensive traveller, Charles collected many Botanical specimens during his journeys. Some of his finds were planted within the park and can still be seen today.

The variety of the park's layout was due largely to the Curator of Vale Park, William Grinsell Burston. Arriving at Liscard Vale as Head Gardener in 1890, he remained in post when the council took over the estate. A renowned horitculturalist, he died at

Vale Park House in 1918, leaving his son, Ernest, to take up the trowel. 1923 saw the construction of the bandstand which continues to host brass band concerts. The bandstand also provided the venue for "Joytime," a children's variety show run by Dorothy Carr and her husband Norman Trafford.

Aunty Dot ran the show for 45 years, and was awarded the British Empire Medal for her work.

Vale House gradually fell into disuse, having been used for many years as a base for park staff.

A Friends of Vale Park campaign was launched to encourage Wirral Borough Council to restore the house.

It re-opened as a community centre in 1993.

GOING CUCKOO

The floral cuckoo clock in Vale Park which was presented to the borough of Wallasey in 1948. Sixteen feet in diameter with a face composed of 20,000 plants, the clock gave cuckoo signals every quarter of an hour. Right, the bandstand in Vale Park in 1959 – it still continues to host brass band concerts today. Below, the War Memorial at Vale Park

RIVER SONGS

Opposite page, the bandstand attracts a large crowd on a sunny day in March 1934, as the ferries sail past in the background

LAMENT FOR A LOST RESORT

BACK in March 1992, writer Nick Hilton went on a story for the Liverpool Daily Post that was close to his heart – but he didn't want to write it.

"NEW BRIGHTON . . . the decline and fall.

"Some time in the next few weeks Joyce Corkish will serve the last meal at Brice's Cafe and surrender the premises to the demolition men. She is dreading that moment. Those who have become cynical about New Brighton's decline – and there are many – might call it the last supper for the last resort.

"Joyce is not among them. She is proud to be the owner of the oldest cafe in what could have once been called downtown New Brighton and just as proud that Brice's Cafe will be the last to close in run-down New Brighton.
"It is very upsetting to have to go; this place has been my life."

That was then. In 1992 Brice's was surrounded by the boarded up and derelict remains of New Brighton's once-thriving cafe society. When Joyce was a teenage waitress in the final years of the resort's heyday, the summertime ferry service from Liverpool would, she then recalled, bring people swarming up Victoria Road like ants.

More than enough business to go around for the likes of Lawton's Cafe, Duffy's Cafe, the Sheffield, Paddy's Snack bar, Billy's Fish and Chip Eat-in-or-Take Away and Maxim's next door but one. The menus then were almost the same:

FISH, CHIPS AND PEAS
STEAK AND KIDNEY PIE AND CHIPS, WHITE
BREAD AND BUTTER CUT CORNER TO CORNER
POTS OF TEA

Yes, pots not JUST a cup. That's how it was then.

Nick recalled that the locals and bus pass day trippers, who made up most of the winter trade, liked what they got at Brice's. The wonderful shortcrust pastry and fish and chips for £2.
The décor had not changed. The straight wooden back chairs and sturdy tables could have been in place the day the premises opened as a dairy cafe in 1884. The checked cotton cloths and the plastic red roses on each table evoked the 1950s.

Once there were photographs on the walls of stage artists who had performed at the Floral, but they were all ruined on the day the orange drink machine exploded.

Back in March 1992 the walls were hung with paintings of New Brighton in the good old days.

No fun at the fair – a sad sight in 1992

Joyce Corkish, owner of Brice's Cafe,
pictured in 1992, just a few weeks
before the business closed.

THE tight-knit coastal town of New Brighton, on Wirral's northern corner facing both the Mersey estuary and the Irish Sea, has a long history of attracting tourists.

In the decades after James Atherton recognised its potential and bought up land to build on, the town grew and grew, becoming a destination of choice for many.

With its beaches stretching away towards Liverpool on one side and the Irish Sea on the other, rows of shops selling fish and chips, cotton candy and New Brighton rock, images of sunny days here are the stuff of memories long cherished by earlier generations.

But like many seaside resorts it faced a steep decline as foreign holidays became cheaper and promised more reliable weather.

Because although the sun always means New Brighton is thronged with visitors, meteorology has proved unable to keep it busy enough. In a bid to combat this decline and somehow engineer a renaissance for the town, the redevelopment of the resort has been an almost non-stop cycle of proposals and grand plans. These combinations of the wildly ambitious and frankly unbelievable have

always, until recently, come aground at the rock of reality or otherwise fallen by the wayside.

Many may remember the Japanese Ocean Dome from the 1990s, and even further back proposals to build all along the Dips – the open space where the Wirral Show used to be held – but which are now considered sacrosanct by locals.

For the last decade or so Liverpool developers Neptune have been the favoured choice of the council to actually do something and seeing it happen. Their plans have at times divided the town whose residents often feel passionately about it.

At the height of the opposition to an earlier incarnation of the current Neptune scheme, house and shop windows around the town hosted posters either for or against the plans.

But despite courting controversy, the developers have stuck doggedly with the town and revised and re-thought their scheme repeatedly, in a bid to please as many people as possible while still being a practical possibility.

Once upon a time they wanted to build on part of the marine lake, which had been largely left to silt up and became all but unusable over the years.

Despite this, a vehement opposition brought that

A NEW NEW BRIGHTON

SUNSHINE is all New Brighton has ever needed to bring in hoards of visitors, writes Liam Murphy.

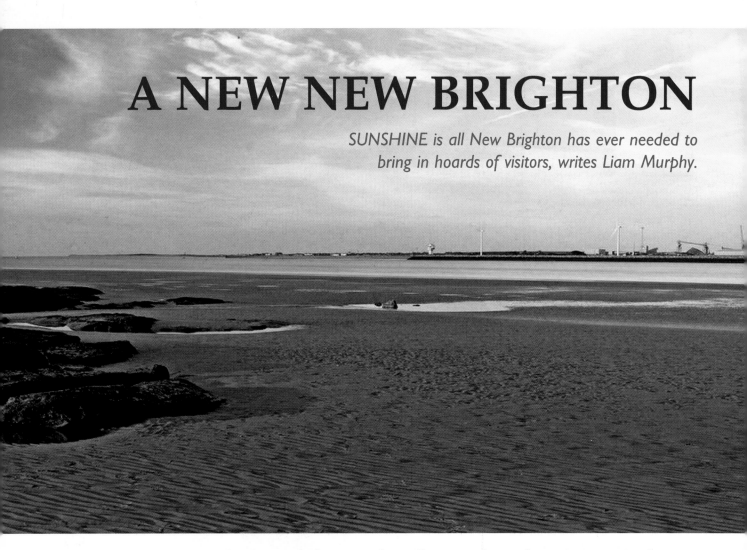

plan to an end with an extraordinary tour de force by local residents at the public inquiry in Wallasey town hall, following a massive publicity campaign against the plan which had even included tying a yellow ribbon around the lake.

In a David versus Goliath-style battle the campaigners defeated the combined forces of developers Neptune and the council in a hard fought legal battle before a planning inspector.

At the time it looked like this spelled the end of the Neptune scheme, but somehow out of the ashes a new vision of how the development could be pushed forward emerged.

A number of the most vocal opponents suddenly found themselves working with Neptune and from this collaboration grew the current incarnation of the £60 million "New New Brighton".

Foremost so far has been the redevelopment of the Floral Pavilion Theatre which has proven to be one of the most eye-catching and attractive buildings to have ever graced that waterfront, in the first phase of the Neptune scheme.

With the theatre's conference facilities set to be complemented by the opening of the 60-bed hotel in the second phase of the development, it is hoped

this will prove to be an alternative attraction for a different type of visitor to the resort.

The second phase of the scheme, being completed this year, will see the always controversial Morrisons by the seaside still in situ, with a six-screen digital 1,100 seater cinema, the hotel, a Lido and shops, bars and restaurants, as well as a newly dredged marine lake for boating and an impressive sailing school building.

The controversy still remains, however, with Neptune facing petitions and complaints about an apartment block which should have been built alongside the Floral Pavilion and they recently wanted to redesign. New Brighton's residents and business people retain their ability to stand up for their town. The new development may never bring back the town's heyday. The massive outdoor pool has long since been demolished and had declined in popularity anyway, the tower is gone, along with the ballroom.

But the new development offers finally a brighter future for a town which had fallen on hard times, it holds out the possibility that people will return to New Brighton for days out which will stick – like rock – in the memory.

Liverpool architect Ken Martin designed the new Floral Pavilion. At the opening in December 2008 he said it was the happiest day of his professional life and one of the best commissions he had worked on.

GUIDING LIGHTS

NEW BRIGHTON always had real vision. BBC Broadcaster Roger Lyon explains why it remains special for him and many others.

THE fact that the Guide Dogs for the Blind Association started in New Brighton is something to be immensely proud of, and is yet another first for Merseyside.

I have always been an animal lover and have raised money for various animal charities over the years. I have also had personal experience of the amazing job that a guide dog can do.

A former colleague of mine was blind and had the use of a dog called Heather. When she had her harness on and she knew she was in work mode, nothing could distract her from enabling her charge to lead as normal a life as possible.

However once she was 'off duty' she reverted to the most wonderful loving pet that it was possible to be. Together they were truly a team, and when the time came for Heather to retire and be replaced by

HEART-WARMING TAIL

The statue celebrating the Guide Dogs for the Blind Association, outside the new Floral Pavilion in New Brighton

'Rodney', it was gratifying to know that people were queuing up to find her a home to enjoy her later years. I have run the London Marathon three times for Guide Dogs, and on one of those years I ran in a dog costume of Floppy ears, tail and shiny nose. On the way to the starting line a woman on the tube said to me: "Have you been running?" and I said, "No, love, I always dress this way."

I eventually raised several thousands of pounds for the charity which continues to provide a lifeline for many sight-impaired people – and to think that it all started in New Brighton.

New Brighton's clown statue on King's Parade, designed by artist Joan Ellis

WELCOME TO NEW BRIGHTON

"New Brighton's residents and business people retain their ability to stand up for their town."

GREAT READS FROM THE HEART OF THE CITY

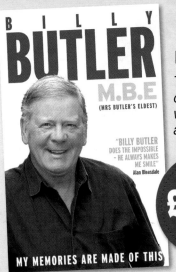

BILLY BUTLER M.B.E.

Tune into a radio show with a difference – Billy's life story, packed with hilarious childhood memories and his love of trivia.

£7.50
FREE p&p (UK)

Only **£2.00**
+£1 p&p (UK)

THE WAY WE WORKED

Unilever, Vernons, Littlewoods, Crawford's, Tate & Lyle, Woolies. Our jobs – our memories.

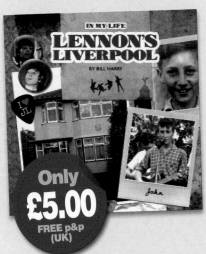

LENNON'S LIVERPOOL

In this book, the magical music landscape of Liverpool through John's early life is explored.

Only **£5.00**
FREE p&p (UK)

Only **£3.99**
+£1 p&p (UK)

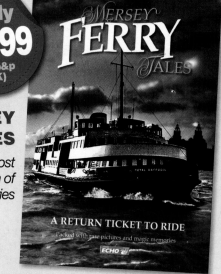

MERSEY FERRY TALES

A ticket to ride on the world's most famous ferry – a unique collection of magic maritime memories

Only **£4.50**
+£1 p&p (UK)

THE McCARTNEY'S – In the Town Where They Were Born

This book, for the first time, goes back to McCartney's roots, unveiling the secrets of his childhood and early life in Liverpool.

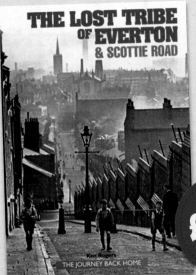

THE LOST TRIBE OF EVERTON & SCOTTIE ROAD

This nostalgic book by Ken Rogers will take you back 'home' into the inner city streets and make you feel proud.

Only **£9.99**
FREE p&p (UK)

SCOTTIE ROAD

The bricks and mortar of Scottie Road may be a memory but the spirit lingers on. Featuring great photographs from the Scottie Press collection and rarely seen historical images from the League of Welldoers' Lee Jones Collection.

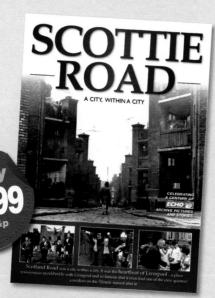

Only £3.99 +£1 p&p (UK)

Only £3.99 +£1 p&p (UK)

LOST CINEMAS OF LIVERPOOL

Book your ticket for a trip down movie memory lane, to a time when Liverpool was a Tinsel Town in its own right and there was a cinema on every corner.

Only £3.99 +£1 p&p (UK)

MERSEY BLITZ

This special publication marks the 70th anniversary of the May blitz, when the Luftwaffe rained bombs, land mines and incendiary devices on Liverpool.

"Are yer dancin'?" "Are yer askin'?"

Send us your stories and you could have a starring role in our next archive special...

THERE was a time when gliding and spinning across the dance floor, under glitter balls and subtle lighting in a myriad of famous venues, was THE number one entertainment activity for every adult on Merseyside.

Did you visit places like the Grafton, Locarno, Orrell Park Ballroom, the Rialto, Peppers on Aubrey Street, Blair Hall on Walton Road, or Reece's in the city centre?

Have you got vivid memories of giant venues like the Tower Ballroom in New Brighton, and St George's Hall, or have you got personal dance tales about smaller district venues that have long since drifted out of our psyche? Have you ever been knocked back on the dance floor after asking: "Are yer dancin'?"

Or were you one of those men with two left feet who stood on the fringe of the floor for hours, terrified to cross the line into that seething mass of swaying and rhythmic inter-action?

We want to hear from you as we prepare a fascinating magazine that will bring back some fantastic memories of the real-life 'Strictly Come Dancing' era. Send your stories and pictures to: Peter Grant, Liverpool Daily Post & Echo, Old Hall Street, Liverpool L69 3EB, or email petergrant@liverpoolecho.co.uk

GOLDEN ERA

Actor Michael Starke has his own fond memories of New Brighton: "As a child I went to New Brighton and it was another world. Getting on that ferry and away – even if only for a day. It could have been another country. Many, many years later I took my own kids to Disneyworld in Florida and my dad was with us and we all sat there, looking around at all the magical things that were there, and I was thinking, 'Isn't this fantastic?' Dad looked up and smiled, but then said: 'Yes, like when you were younger, when we had New Brighton. We always had New Brighton'".
Picture by Bob Bird

PARADISE LOST

This magazine has taken you on a sentimental journey back to the days when New Brighton reigned supreme as Merseyside's very own magic kingdom.

It's the 1950s and the sun is going down on another fantastic day out. The last Ferry is signalling its impending departure back towards the waiting Liver Birds, and the beach is beginning to empty like a football stadium spilling its mighty crowd back into the real world.

The bags are packed, the deckchairs are being returned, and the coats and scarves suggest that the blue skies over the Wirral would now be giving way to clouds of uncertainty.

New Brighton's famous Tower would be demolished, the Pier would be swallowed by a raging storm, and Liverpool's very own sunshine paradise would now become a seaside postcard memory. But what a memory, and what a place. We will never forget the way it was, and we all dream that New Brighton will rise again as some long overdue investment opens up a string of new possibilities for our special resort 'over the water'.